DON'T BE STUPID!

A PRODIGAL STORY

DON'T BE STUPID!

A PRODIGAL STORY

Craig W. Hagin

CONTENTS

INTRODUCTION

So many times we read a Bible story, agree that it's a good story, and then move on. But what did that really do for us? Did it help us? Did we feel better after reading the story? Often our answer is probably "no." We just don't understand the story the way Jesus' audience did.

That's what this book is all about. I want to take one of Jesus' stories—the parable of the prodigal son—and really dissect it. You may be familiar with it already, but I want to help you see it as you never have before.

It's much more than just a story of a son who lost his way. It's a story about a son who didn't understand his father's love. It's about a brother's jealousy. It's about a pigpen and the choices we make. It's about you and me fulfilling our God-given destiny. But ultimately, it's a story that shows us the true love of God. God is always for us. He is always with us. And He always wants us to come back to Him.

LUKE 15:11–32

¹¹ *Then He said: "A certain man had two sons.* ¹² *And the younger of them said to his father, 'Father, give me the portion of goods that falls to me.' So he divided to them his livelihood.* ¹³ *And not many days after, the younger son gathered all together, journeyed to a far country, and there wasted his possessions with prodigal living.* ¹⁴ *But when he had spent all, there arose a severe famine in that land, and he began to be in want.* ¹⁵ *Then he went and joined himself to a citizen of that country, and he sent him into his fields to feed swine.* ¹⁶ *And he would gladly have filled his stomach with the pods that the swine ate, and no one gave him anything.*

¹⁷ *"But when he came to himself, he said, 'How many of my father's hired servants have bread enough and to spare, and I perish with hunger!* ¹⁸ *I will arise and go to my father, and will say to him, "Father, I have sinned against heaven and before you,* ¹⁹ *and I am no longer worthy to be called your son. Make me like one of your hired servants."'*

²⁰ *"And he arose and came to his father. But when he was still a great way off, his father saw him and had compassion, and ran and fell on his neck and kissed him.* ²¹ *And the son said to him, 'Father, I have sinned against heaven and in your sight, and am no longer worthy to be called your son.'*

[22] *"But the father said to his servants, 'Bring out the best robe and put it on him, and put a ring on his hand and sandals on his feet. [23] And bring the fatted calf here and kill it, and let us eat and be merry; [24] for this my son was dead and is alive again; he was lost and is found.' And they began to be merry.*

[25] "Now his older son was in the field. And as he came and drew near to the house, he heard music and dancing. [26] So he called one of the servants and asked what these things meant. [27] And he said to him, 'Your brother has come, and because he has received him safe and sound, your father has killed the fatted calf.'

[28] "But he was angry and would not go in. Therefore his father came out and pleaded with him. [29] So he answered and said to his father, 'Lo, these many years I have been serving you; I never transgressed your commandment at any time; and yet you never gave me a young goat, that I might make merry with my friends. [30] But as soon as this son of yours came, who has devoured your livelihood with harlots, you killed the fatted calf for him.'

[31] "And he said to him, 'Son, you are always with me, and all that I have is yours. [32] It was right that we should make merry and be glad, for your brother was dead and is alive again, and was lost and is found.'"

Chapter 1

THE PATH TO THE PIGPEN

"The younger son gathered all together, journeyed to a far country, and there wasted his possessions with prodigal living."
—Luke 15:13

What does it take to become a prodigal? Have you ever thought about that? I don't believe the prodigal son in Luke chapter 15 just woke up one morning and decided to take his inheritance and leave the country. He didn't eat too much pizza one night and suddenly start packing.

No. I believe there was a process that led up to this son leaving his father's household. And I believe that process started with one word. It's the same word that causes many of us to set in motion a string of bad decisions—decisions that ultimately take us places we don't want to go. The word I'm talking about is *frustration*.

Now before we go any further, let's give the two sons in our story names to keep things from getting confusing. We'll call the older son John and the younger son Steve.

We aren't told exactly what happened to cause Steve to become frustrated and leave. It's possible he just didn't like his dad's rules. But I believe there was probably a rivalry between the two brothers. Look at John's reaction when Steve came back. Luke 15:28 says he was angry. He certainly wasn't happy to see his little brother.

It's possible that Steve was jealous of his older brother. In Jewish culture, the oldest son received the majority of the inheritance. The oldest son was the one exalted by others.

Maybe little Stevie felt as though he could never live up to his older brother's reputation. People may have said to him, "Why can't you be like John? He's a better student than you are. He's a better athlete." Over time, words like these would have only fueled Steve's frustration.

BAD INFLUENCE

When people are frustrated, they rarely seek wise counsel. The truth is, they really don't want good advice. They're looking for people who will tell them what they want to hear—people who will agree with them. They find someone else who is frustrated with the person *they're* frustrated with. Usually, this is the guy who's never moved out of his parents' basement and still plays with his original Star Wars action figures!

In Steve's case, he probably found a buddy or two his own age. Then he and his "advisors" talked about his frustrations again and again. That's what Jesus did, right? He sat with his disciples and talked about how wrong everyone else was.

No! That's not being a doer of God's Word. Jesus never did this. However, it's possible that Steve did. It's also likely that Steve's friends encouraged him to ask for his part of the family inheritance and leave town. Among themselves, they worked out a scenario of how great everything would be once Steve got away from John and out from under his father's jurisdiction.

WRONG THINKING

Why was Steve so willing to consider leaving? He was frustrated, and frustration causes us to think about change. I'm sure Steve thought, "If I leave the house, it will be a whole lot better. The next country over has nice beaches and pretty girls. I can just sit on the beach, watch the waves come up, and hire guys to go and fish for me. I can afford to do whatever I want. Why should I live here with my dad and my frustrating brother?"

Unfortunately for Steve, being frustrated with something—or someone—does not mean it's time to leave.

> **WE SHOULD NEVER INITIATE CHANGE OUT OF FRUSTRATION.**

A lot of times, frustration is a sign that we have a personal issue we need to get rid of. Of course, if God is leading us to do something different, we should follow His leading. But we should never initiate change out of frustration.

Many people don't realize that if we don't deal with what's bothering us, frustration will only grow. As it piles up, we'll become more and more irritable. Eventually, we'll become

> **OUR FRUSTRATION DOESN'T MEAN THAT OTHER PEOPLE NEED TO SHIFT THEIR WHOLE WAY OF THINKING TO CODDLE US.**

frustrated with everyone around us—friends, family, and co-workers. But our frustration doesn't mean that other people need to shift their whole way of thinking to coddle us. It's our issue, not someone else's. Unfortunately for Steve, he didn't figure this out until he'd left home and wasted his inheritance.

WHO ARE YOU HANGING WITH?

Now to be honest, I don't think Steve ever intended to become a prodigal. I don't believe he meant to recklessly waste his entire inheritance. I believe he just wanted to go out and make a name for himself. When he left, he probably kept his morality for awhile. But before too long he found himself surrounded by all the wrong people.

> **»»THE PEOPLE YOU HANG AROUND CAN CHANGE YOUR FUTURE.**

You see, who you hang around is very important. First Corinthians 15:33 says, *"Do not be deceived: 'Evil company corrupts good habits.'"* The *New Century Version* says it like this: *"Do not be fooled: 'Bad friends will ruin good habits.'"* In other words, the people you hang around can change your future. If you want to be a champion, hang around champions. If you want to be a loser, hang around losers.

For Steve, it's likely that the people he chose to hang around—both before and after leaving home—negatively affected his lifestyle. They led him on a downward spiral that eventually landed him in the pigpen.

HOW DO WE AVOID THE PIGPEN?

We can see that Steve's frustration led him down a path where he never intended to be. By looking at his example, I believe we can avoid the same mistake.

We must look honestly at ourselves. Have we allowed bitterness and strife to creep in? Are we allowing issues to boil and fester? If so, we have to deal with these things.

See, frustration is not faith. When we're standing in faith, we're going to have peace. When we're standing in faith, we're going to look to our Heavenly Father rather than at our circumstances.

To stay in faith, we must decide to quit letting things bother us. First Peter 5:7 (NLT) says, *"Give all your worries and cares to God, for he cares about* you." We have to learn to let go and give everything to God. If we don't, then before we know it, we'll become like the prodigal son. We'll walk out the door and end up at the same destination he did.

> **»»WE HAVE TO LEARN TO LET GO AND GIVE EVERYTHING TO GOD.**

That's what the devil wants. John 10:10 says that he comes to steal, kill, and destroy. And often that destruction starts with a thought. But we cannot let piddly situations alter our destiny like Steve did. God has a plan and purpose for each of our lives. And when we stop trying to become somebody and just let Him work through us, He will give us all we need. He will exalt us and bring us satisfaction.

Just look at King David. He was the youngest of all his brothers. He was the least of them all. Yet he ended up being exalted above them all (see First Samuel chapter 16). Why? Because the Lord looks at the heart (1 Sam. 16:7). That means if we'll set our hearts right, God will exalt us to the place we need to be.

> **» IF WE'LL SET OUR HEARTS RIGHT, GOD WILL EXALT US TO THE PLACE WE NEED TO BE.**

I encourage you, check your heart today. Get quiet and let the Holy Spirit speak to you. Are there adjustments you need to make? Are there frustrations you need to let go of? Don't wait! Let go of those things right now and turn your heart over to the Lord. It's time to get off the path to the pigpen and start walking in God's blessings!

THINK IT OVER

1. Why is frustration such a bad thing for us as believers?

2. Are there people or areas of your life you're frustrated with right now? Explain.

3. Who are you hanging out with—people who give you wise counsel or people who fuel your frustration? What do you think you need to change in this area?

4. Are you ready to let God exalt you to the place you need to be? Take a moment right now and turn all of your frustrations over to Him. Trust Him to place you on His path for you, and then walk in His peace.

Chapter 2

IT'S ALL ABOUT ME

"And the younger of them said to his father, 'Father, give me the portion of goods that falls to me.' So he divided to them his livelihood. And not many days after, the younger son gathered all together, [and] journeyed to a far country."
—Luke 15:12–13

One of the things that stands out to me in the story of the prodigal son is that Steve—the prodigal—had some real guts. Normally, sons did not receive their inheritance until after their father had passed away. But Steve asked for his portion early. By doing so, he was basically telling his father, "I wish you were dead."

This was unheard of in Steve's day! The father was still using his possessions. It wasn't just money. We're talking about cattle and land. But everything he had, he just gave to his sons.

Now, maybe he didn't actually give Steve a herd of cows. Maybe he said, "These cows are worth $30,000, so I'll give you your portion in cash and you can take that." But what's amazing is that this father was willing to grant a request that most fathers never would. And he let his son go.

A FATHER'S LOVE

It's important to note here that when the father let Steve leave, it did not mean that was his will. I'm sure the father would have preferred to have his son stay nearby. I know I would have if that had been me.

Steve's father didn't kick him out either. He didn't come in one day and say, "Steve, you're just lazy. All you do is sit around. I'm tired of having you here. You need to go to another kingdom, because you're messing mine up." He may have thought some of these things, but he was willing to accept his son the way he was. His love never changed.

Had Steve realized this, his attitude may have been different. But he selfishly wanted things his own way, and he left with his inheritance. Essentially, Steve disowned his entire family. But he didn't stop there. He also decided to leave the Promised Land and live in a foreign place. He completely removed himself from his dad's authority and from the Word he had been taught.

You see, Steve could have taken his inheritance and stayed nearby. His dad obviously had some land. He could have built his own little kingdom—Steve Land—with Pete the Pig as mascot. He could have worked in conjunction with his family to benefit everyone.

However, Steve didn't want to move to another part of the family's land. He wasn't interested in working together with his family to grow a bigger, better farm. He was more concerned about doing things his way.

MY WAY OR GOD'S WAY

I think we all have opportunities to do things our own way. Personally, I've had opportunities to go out and start my own ministry. And I could have been successful at it. But Craig's Bible Church wouldn't have been God's plan. It wouldn't have been God's best for my family or Kenneth Hagin Ministries.

The truth is, it's not about me. It's really not about any of us. It's not about our plan, our way, or our rules. It's not about exalting ourselves. It's about helping and exalting others—being a blessing. We're supposed to go out and follow Jesus' example.

> **》》IT'S NOT ABOUT EXALTING OURSELVES. IT'S ABOUT HELPING AND EXALTING OTHERS— BEING A BLESSING.**

What did Jesus do? Acts 10:38 says He went about doing good. He went around loving people—even those who weren't the most godly or lovable. Remember Zaccheus, the tax collector? No one wanted to hang out with him. But Jesus told him, "I'm coming to your house today" (Luke 19:1–10). From that moment, Zaccheus' life changed completely.

Just like Jesus, we should make our goal going out and changing people's lives—seeing them born again. We should be lights in a dark world. That means we need to turn our eyes off ourselves—off our needs—and on to other people. We have to forget about ourselves. Forget the "I" mentality. And really, forget the "we" mentality too. What we really need is a "He" mentality. Jesus does the work through us. *He* leads us. *He* carries us. *He's* in control. It's all about Him.

Matthew 6:33 tells us, *"Seek the Kingdom of God above all else, and live righteously, and he will give you everything you need"* (NLT). When we take care of God's Kingdom— when we focus on doing the works of Jesus—the Word promises that God has our back. However, when we choose to focus on ourselves like Steve did, that "I" mentality could very well land us in the middle of a pig stall.

YOU DECIDE

You may say, "Well, my God wouldn't let me wind up in the pigpen." Yes, He would. God *is* loving and merciful, but if Steve were alive today, he'd end up in the same place. Why? For the reason I just mentioned. God loves us. And He's given us the ability to make our own choices.

Deuteronomy 30:19 says, *"I have set before you life and death, blessing and cursing; therefore choose life."* We can choose life, but we can also choose death. God

> **GOD LOVES US. AND HE'S GIVEN US THE ABILITY TO MAKE OUR OWN CHOICES.**

doesn't force us to do anything. He doesn't hold us hostage. He allows us to make our own decisions.

Think about salvation. The Bible is clear that Jesus is knocking on the door of our hearts (Rev. 3:20). If we'll open the door and let Him in, He'll dwell with us. But we don't have to let Him in. We have the right to accept or reject Him.

When I was a kid, I had books filled with different instructions that allowed the reader to develop the story. For example, "You're standing at a door. If you want to go in the door, turn to page 23. If you want to keep walking down the hall, turn to page 85." It would go on and on. You made your own choices, and with every choice you changed the story. Sometimes you picked the right way and sometimes you picked the wrong way.

It's the same in life. We can choose to go our own way or we can go God's way. Some people have the wrong idea.

They believe God's going to bless us no matter which way we choose. But God doesn't have to bless *our* choices. Does He *want* to bless us? Yes. But His blessings come when we choose to follow Him.

> >> HIS BLESSINGS COME WHEN WE CHOOSE TO FOLLOW HIM.

WHAT ARE YOU FOCUSING ON?

What we do in life—what we choose to focus on—changes us. It's not just about existing. It's about making our mark in this world and making it a better place. It's about going out and doing something to help people. But it starts with forgetting about ourselves. It starts with trusting in and focusing on the Lord.

> >> IT'S ABOUT MAKING OUR MARK IN THIS WORLD AND MAKING IT A BETTER PLACE.

Proverbs 3:5–6 says, *"Trust in the Lord with all your heart, and lean not on your own understanding; in all your ways acknowledge Him, and HE SHALL DIRECT YOUR PATHS."* When we decide to put our trust in the Lord and focus on Him, that's when He directs our paths. But when we choose to focus on circumstances and troubles like Steve did, we give the devil an opportunity to slip in. That's when we lose our way.

Remember when Peter saw Jesus walking on the water in Matthew chapter 14? He asked, "Can I come out there with You" (v. 28)? As long as Peter's mind was stayed on Jesus, he didn't have trouble walking on the water. But when he started looking at the waves and the wind, he began to sink (vv. 29–30).

It's the same with us today. We can't focus on what's happening around us or we'll sink deep into the mud. We have to focus on one thing and one thing only—Jesus Christ. *He's* the answer.

We've got to say goodbye to the "I" mentality and be open, willing vessels for Jesus. Doing things our way can be costly. Steve found that out. But doing things God's way always pays.

> ⟫**DOING THINGS GOD'S WAY ALWAYS PAYS.**

THINK IT OVER

1. Why is selfishness such a bad thing? Are there areas of your life where you've been selfish?

2. Whose example are we supposed to follow? What did that Person do when He was alive on the earth?

3. List three ways you can "do good" to those around you.

4. What are you focused on today? Are you looking to the Lord or at your circumstances? Decide right now that you're going to trust the Lord—no matter what.

Chapter 3

WHAT YOU DESERVE?
I DON'T THINK SO!

"He came to himself."
—Luke 15:17

Did you ever notice that when you have money, everyone wants to be your friend? It's amazing. If you win the $425 million Powerball lottery, you'll meet people you never knew existed. You'll have instant popularity, because everyone wants a piece of your winnings. But what happens when the money is gone?

Our prodigal, Steve, found out the hard way. When he needed friends the most, they'd all left him. Sure, they partied it up together for awhile. It was all fun for a season. But eventually Steve found himself in the pigpen—penniless and alone.

UNCLEAN PIGS

For Steve, the pigpen situation was about as bad as it could get. The Jews whom Jesus told this story to would have understood this. In their culture, the pig is an unclean animal—not fit to eat. And Steve was working with them as a professional pig feeder!

To make matters worse, he was so hungry that even the pigs' food looked appetizing.

> **LUKE 15:16 (NLT)**
> *16* The young man became so hungry that even the pods he was feeding the pigs looked good to him. But no one gave him anything.

I don't know about you, but I would not want to eat what pigs eat. However, Steve had no other options. He was out of money.

Thankfully, while he was wallowing around in the mud, something happened. Luke 15:17 says Steve *"came to himself."* This young prodigal had a mud-pit moment. He began to remember his father and how good he was—even to his servants. And he realized he would rather go back home and become one of those servants than stay with the pigs and starve.

> **LUKE 15:17–19**
> *17* "But when he came to himself, he said, 'How many of my father's hired servants have bread enough and to spare, and I perish with hunger!

18 I will arise and go to my father, and will say to him, "Father, I have sinned against heaven and before you,

19 and I am no longer worthy to be called your son. Make me like one of your hired servants." ' "

Steve was finally ready to return home to his father.

STOP WALLOWING IN THE PIGPEN

Although Steve came to himself, many people today do not. Or it takes them a really long time to do so. I know people who were once on fire for God, but they are now wallowing in the pigpen—and have been for decades. They're doing only what's needed to get by. Many are so used to living with pigs that it's not even a big deal anymore.

I'm talking about people with a call of God on their lives. They let some sort of resentment or wrong belief into their hearts, and it changed their destiny. Some are in jail. Others are atheists and want nothing to do with God. They're in the pigpen.

I know other people who look like a million bucks on the outside. But on the inside, they're hurting like crazy. They're in the mud mentally. They may have rededicated their lives to God, but they've banished themselves to the pigpen. They think they don't deserve any better—that they don't deserve to have good things—because of what they did in the past.

The truth is, Christianity is not about what we deserve. If it were, we'd all be dead because of our sins (Eph. 2:1). But Ephesians 2:4–5 says

> »**CHRISTIANITY IS NOT ABOUT WHAT WE DESERVE.**

that together with Christ, God made us alive! Jesus took our punishment—what we deserved—and gave us His love, joy, health, and peace.

Remember the woman the scribes and Pharisees brought to Jesus in John chapter 8? She'd been caught in the act of adultery and they wanted to stone her. But Jesus said, " *'He who is without sin among you, let him throw a stone at her first'* " (v. 7).

> »**WE'VE ALL BEEN IN PIGPEN SITUATIONS.**

No one threw a stone. Why? Because we've *all* sinned. We've all done things that weren't the best. We've all been in pigpen situations. But we don't have to stay there! We can get out.

God is able and willing to pick us up out of whatever we've put ourselves into. I don't care how bad it seems. I don't care if we're under six feet of mud—beneath the pigpen. God has provided a way for us.

Just look at Paul and Silas. In Acts chapter 16 they were in an impossible situation, in jail. I'm not talking about a jail with cable TV. I'm talking about a dungeon. They were chained to the wall and were hurting after being beaten with rods. To make things worse, it looked like they were going to be killed the next day. It was a bad situation.

Most people would be griping and complaining. But Acts 16:25 says, *"At midnight Paul and Silas were praying and singing hymns to God."* These men weren't focused on their situation. They were praying and singing praises to God! Look what happened next.

ACTS 16:26

26 Suddenly there was a great earthquake, so that the foundations of the prison were shaken; and immediately all the doors were opened and everyone's chains were loosed.

Paul and Silas knew they could trust God. And He delivered not only them but everyone in the prison!

IT'S NOT TOO LATE

Just as He did for Paul and Silas, God can turn things around for us—even when we're facing the worst possible circumstances. Someone may say, "But I've messed my life up so bad. I just can't get any better. God doesn't want me."

>> **GOD CAN TURN THINGS AROUND FOR US—EVEN WHEN WE'RE FACING THE WORST POSSIBLE CIRCUMSTANCES.**

Stop listening to the devil's lies! The reason your life is a mess is that the devil is out to destroy you. He wants to steal your life from you (John 10:10). And he wants you to think that you deserve to stay in the pigpen for the rest of your days. He may even be trying to tell you to end your life—that your life is worthless.

Your life is not worthless! I know it can sometimes feel as if you're in a situation where you can't get back up. You feel like you're too far away from God and that there's no one who can help you. But what's in your past doesn't matter. What other people

>> **WHAT'S IN YOUR PAST DOESN'T MATTER. WHAT OTHER PEOPLE THINK DOESN'T MATTER. THE BIBLE SAYS THAT GOD LOVES YOU UNCONDITIONALLY.**

think doesn't matter. The Bible says that God loves you unconditionally. Nothing can separate you from His love (Rom. 8:38–39).

Now, it is possible for you to separate yourself from the Lord because you feel you're not worthy. "This is what I deserve." "This is my lot in life." "God is doing this to punish me." Have you ever found yourself saying these words? That's what I call a mud-pit mentality. And that kind of thinking will keep you away from God and wallowing in the mud with the pigs.

The truth is, God is always there for you. He's not trying to punish you. And no matter what you've done—even if you've got a long laundry list of sins—you can come boldly to His throne, knowing that He won't reject you. That's why Jesus came, isn't it? John 3:16 says, *"God so loved the world that he gave his one and only Son"* (NIV). God never stopped loving the world, even when it wouldn't accept Him. And He has never stopped loving you either.

>> **GOD IS ALWAYS THERE FOR YOU.**

THE FATHER'S LOVE

We see this unconditional love that the Father has for us in the story of the prodigal son. As Steve began his trek back to see his father, he thought he'd just live as a servant. That's what he wanted. (Interestingly, if Steve had had this attitude in the old days, he would never have ended up in the pigpen.) But look at what happened when his father saw him.

LUKE 15:20–24

20 "But when he was still a great way off, his father saw him and had compassion, and ran and fell on his neck and kissed him.

21 And the son said to him, 'Father, I have sinned against heaven and in your sight, and am no longer worthy to be called your son.'

22 "But the father said to his servants, 'Bring out the best robe and put it on him, and put a ring on his hand and sandals on his feet.

23 And bring the fatted calf here and kill it, and let us eat and be merry;

24 for this my son was dead and is alive again; he was lost and is found.' And they began to be merry."

Steve's father ran to him when he saw him. And he didn't just give him the position of a servant; he reinstated him as a son. Think about this for a moment. This son had basically disowned his father and his entire family. But the father ran to him anyway and ordered the servants to bring the best they had. His son was "alive" again!

> **GOD SAYS, "YOU'RE WORTH MORE THAN THAT."**

Our Father God is the same way. When we come back to Him—or even when we just finally give all our issues to Him—He runs to meet us. He comes to us and says, "I'm glad you're back. You're not going to live as a servant. You're going to live as a son or daughter."

The Bible says we are children of God (1 John 3:2). And that's how God treats us—not as servants. God says, "You're worth more than that." With Him, there's no barely getting blessed. It's 110 percent—more than enough.

IT'S PARTY TIME

After the father in our story welcomed his son back, the Bible says *"they began to be merry"* (Luke 15:24). In other words, they began to party. The father told his servants to kill the fatted calf—the biggest calf out there! It didn't matter how much money they spent, because his son had come home.

If a natural father was this excited when his child came home, how much more excited do you think our Heavenly Father gets when a son or daughter returns to Him? Luke 15:7 (NLT) says, *"There is more joy in heaven over one lost sinner who repents and returns to God than over ninety-nine others who are righteous and haven't strayed away!"*

There's nothing like coming back to our Father! We've all had pigpen experiences where it's miserable. Everything goes wrong and nothing seems right. But praise God, when we come back to Him, He welcomes us with open arms.

> »START SEEING YOURSELF TODAY THE WAY GOD SEES YOU.

SEE YOURSELF AS GOD SEES YOU

Start seeing yourself today the way God sees you. He doesn't see you as a loser. He doesn't see you as someone who can't do anything right. He sees you as someone who's always more than a conqueror in Christ. He sees you as a winner, even when you feel like you're a loser.

Jesus didn't die on the cross for a worthless person. He didn't die the way He did for you to be depressed or so the devil could whip you every day. He didn't die for you so you could stay in the pigpen. Jesus died on the cross for you because He loves you. He gave His own life so you could have an abundant life—a life of freedom, healing, and prosperity. And He is not just your Savior ultimately. Jesus is your Savior in any situation you're going through.

>> THE ONLY THING KEEPING YOU DOWN RIGHT NOW IS YOU.

If you're in the pigpen, I encourage you—don't stay there. Instead, use it as an opportunity to change your destiny. Come to yourself! Regardless of what you've done, God thinks you're still amazing. The only thing keeping you down right now is you.

If you've fallen, who cares? It's time to rise and shake off the mud-pit mentality! It's time to decide, "I don't want to live like this anymore. I want to feel different." God, the Father, loves you. He wants you to get up—and He's right there, ready to help you.

>> GOD ACCEPTS YOU. HE SAYS YOU'RE WORTHY.

No matter what the people around you say—no matter how they act—God accepts you. He says you're worthy. Turn to Him. With Him by your side, you have everything you need to get past everything you've done. It's time to get out of the mud and party with Him! Your future is bright!

THINK IT OVER

1. What's the worst situation you've ever found yourself in? (For Steve, it was the pigpen.) What did you do in that situation? What could you have done differently?

2. Is Christianity about getting what we deserve? Why or why not?

3. Have you banished yourself to the pigpen in certain areas of your life? Why?

4. Find one scripture in the Bible that talks about God's love for you. Write it down and speak it aloud every day. God is waiting for you with open arms. He loves you. No matter where you've been or where you are now, turn to Him.

Chapter 4

RULES VS. RELATIONSHIP: OLDER-SON SYNDROME

"Now his older son was in the field. And as he came and
drew near to the house, he heard music and dancing.
So he called one of the servants and asked
what these things meant. And he said to him,
'Your brother has come, and . . . your father has killed
the fatted calf.' But he was angry and would not go in."
—Luke 15:25–28

The story of the prodigal son is about more than a guy who ended up in a pigpen and eventually returned home. Steve definitely had heart issues—we've seen that. But his older brother also had some problems. Remember, we're calling the older brother John to keep things simple.

As the story goes, John was out in the field doing his chores—being the good son he'd always been—when he heard music and dancing (Luke 15:25). He wondered what was going on. A servant told him, "Your brother's home!"

If John loved his brother, I think he would have been pretty excited to see him. I've seen brothers who haven't seen each other in a long time who could hardly wait to be reunited.

John, however, became angry. He was mad because his dad was having a party for Steve—the prodigal—and not for him. Look at what he said:

LUKE 15:29–30

29 "So he answered and said to his father, 'Lo, these many years I have been serving you; I never transgressed your commandment at any time; and yet you never gave me a young goat, that I might make merry with my friends.

30 But as soon as this son of yours came, who has devoured your livelihood with harlots, you killed the fatted calf for him.' "

John was the son who'd always done everything right. That's what he told his father. But in this moment, he shows us that we can do everything right and still be wrong.

Jesus talked about this quite a bit in reference to the Pharisees and Sadducees. They were trying to live by the rules instead of from their relationship with the Father. And this is where John missed it too. He complained to his father, "I've always been the good son. I've always followed the rules. But you never even gave me a goat

> »WE CAN DO EVERYTHING RIGHT AND STILL BE WRONG.

so I could party with my friends." Notice what the father said in response.

LUKE 15:31–32

31 "And he said to him, 'Son, you are always with me, and all that I have is yours.

32 It was right that we should make merry and be glad, for your brother was dead and is alive again, and was lost and is found.' "

The father basically said, "Well, if you wanted to have a party, why didn't you? All that I have is yours." What did he mean by that? Let's look back a little in this story.

LUKE 15:12

12 "And the younger of them said to his father, 'Father, give me the portion of goods that falls to me.' So he divided to THEM his livelihood."

Notice the word *them*. The younger son took his portion and left. Everything that remained actually belonged to the older son, including that fatted calf!

When the father said "all that I have is yours," he meant it literally. He'd already given John his inheritance. John could have killed a fatted calf *every day* and had a party! They might have run out of calves that way, but the fact is, he could have done it!

> **JESUS ALREADY CAME AND DIED ON THE CROSS SO THAT WE COULD HAVE AN ABUNDANT LIFE.**

Many believers act the same way the older son did. They gripe and complain, saying, "God, You need to give me something else." But Jesus already came and died on the cross so that we could have an abundant life. He's already provided everything we'll ever need. However, to enjoy those things, we must keep our focus on our relationship with Him.

DON'T MESS UP YOUR BLESSING

I think the father's final words to John in Luke 15:32 also reveal something to us. He told his older son, "You're getting upset when you should be rejoicing. Your brother was dead and is alive again."

I've seen this happen again and again—even in the church. A person goes out and does all sorts of wrong things. When that person comes back home, someone has an issue with him or her. The one who never left becomes jealous, because people seem more concerned about the one who returned than anyone else. And the one who never left says, "*I'm* the one who stayed and did right."

It's not about getting attention. It's about love. It's about caring for our brothers and sisters in Christ. When we become upset and angry because others are getting blessed, we're just messing up our *own* blessing.

Instead of getting mad, we must decide to rejoice with the one returning home— the one returning to the Father. Praise God! That person is getting his life straightened out. It's not about all the

> **WE MUST DECIDE TO REJOICE WITH THE ONE RETURNING HOME.**

things he used to do. It's not about how he ended up in the pigpen. Those things don't matter, because God is not keeping score. When a person comes back to Him, He washes all his sins away.

That's why we must rejoice with those who return. That's why the father in our story told his oldest son, "You should be rejoicing." Steve had come home. He'd returned to the father. He'd gotten his life straightened out.

Sadly, John was more concerned about the "stuff" than about his brother returning home. But if our God supplies us with more than enough of what we need, why are we worried about a little bit of stuff here and there? Why are we worried about someone else getting blessed? It's because we've grabbed hold of the "I'm better than you" mentality. The truth is, we aren't any better just because we didn't go off on the wrong path.

Maybe you've never experienced the pigpen for yourself. Hopefully, you never will. But even if you haven't, it's still good to think about how you'd want to be treated if you *were* in that situation. What would you want your father to do if you were Steve?

UNCONDITIONAL LOVE

God is a God of love. When we understand that love, it will change our lives and thought patterns. It will change the way we treat people.

> **GOD IS A GOD OF LOVE.**

It's not about hate. We can't *hate* people into the Kingdom. But we *can* love people into the Kingdom.

It's not about what someone has done. It's not about the dinner in the pigpen. It's not about that person's wrong choices. It's about him coming to himself and returning to the Father.

In our story, John had an opportunity to become the one most like his father. But he never put himself in Steve's shoes. And he missed the biggest lesson he should have learned—to love people regardless of their faults. God is full of love, compassion, mercy, forgiveness, and grace. And if we're going to be like Him, then we must have those attributes too. We have to love people in spite of their issues. Look at what Jesus said in Mark chapter 12.

MARK 12:30–31

30 "'And you shall love the Lord your God with all your heart, with all your soul, with all your mind, and with all your strength.' This is the first commandment.

31 And the second, like it, is this: 'YOU SHALL LOVE YOUR NEIGHBOR AS YOURSELF.' There is no other commandment greater than these."

You may say, "I don't think I can show unconditional love to everyone around me." It's not about doing things in your own strength. It's not about *your* love. It's about Christ's unconditional love coming through you.

Now, I'm going to be honest. You're going to mess up sometimes. We all have flesh to deal with. Just don't get stuck like the older brother in our story did. Be quick to recognize when you've missed it and say, "God, I'm sorry. I shouldn't be like that."

> ❯❯ IT'S NOT ABOUT YOUR LOVE. IT'S ABOUT CHRIST'S UNCONDITIONAL LOVE COMING THROUGH YOU.

If you'll do that—if you'll trust God and look to His love on the inside—you'll be a light to this dark and hurting world. And you'll find that the Lord's blessings will overtake you in greater ways than you have ever imagined.

THINK IT OVER

1. Have you ever found yourself in a situation like the older son in our story? How did you react?

2. Why is relationship more important than rules when it comes to our Heavenly Father?

3. Why is it so important for us to love people regardless of their faults?

4. Do you find it hard to love others unconditionally? If so, list three scriptures you can meditate on to strengthen your love walk.

Chapter 5

GET OUT OF YOUR STUPID PLACE

"Let this mind be in you which was also in Christ Jesus."
—Philippians 2:5

I see people all the time—young people especially—who have so much potential. Yet they're struggling. They've made choices they shouldn't have made and are in places they shouldn't be in. They've put themselves in their own little pigpen—just like the prodigal son.

Sadly, they won't come to themselves. They won't listen to wise counsel. They aren't following my number one rule: "Don't be stupid." I say that to be funny, but it's true. Why be stupid? Why stay in bondage in the pigpen when you can live in so much more?

> **IT'S TIME TO GET OUT OF YOUR STUPID PLACE, GET UP, AND MOVE FORWARD.**

It's because you've developed a mud-pit mentality. You're not thinking right. It's time to get out of your stupid place, get up, and move forward. In other words, get out of your own mind and get the mind of Christ. Philippians 2:5 says, *"Let this mind be in you which was also in Christ Jesus."* What does that mean? It means you need to get in the Word and begin to think like Jesus. You have to let Him dominate you. Why? Because in Him, you have a lot of benefits you don't have on your own.

USE THE BENEFITS

The benefits we have in Christ won't do us any good if we don't know about them or use them. Let me give you an example of what I mean. I was looking through my desk at work one day and found a gift card to a gas station. It had been there for awhile. I guessed that it probably had $25 on it. But when I checked it, there was $100 on it. I could have used that multiple times to buy fuel, but I just left it sitting there. I didn't use it!

> ❯❯ **THE BENEFITS WE HAVE IN CHRIST WON'T DO US ANY GOOD IF WE DON'T KNOW ABOUT THEM OR USE THEM.**

As believers, we're the same way a lot of times. We don't realize how much God wants to bless us. We don't realize there are benefits we have in Christ that are just sitting on the table unused. My grandfather Kenneth E. Hagin always said that the number one reason people don't get their needs met is that they don't know the Word. When we're facing trials—when we're depressed and going through bad stuff—we have to know what the Word says. We have to know that Jesus is the answer and that we have amazing benefits in Him.

What are these benefits? Let me list a few.

In Christ all of our needs are met (Phil. 4:19).

》》》》

In Christ we're healed (1 Peter 2:24).

》》》》

In Christ we're more than conquerors (Rom. 8:37).

》》》》

In Christ we're victorious (1 Cor. 15:57).

》》》》

In Christ we have joy that other people don't have
(John 16:24; Phil. 4:4; 1 Peter 1:8).

》》》》

In Christ we have peace that passes all understanding
(John 14:27; Phil. 4:7).

》》》》

In Christ there's nothing we can't accomplish (Phil. 4:13).

》》》》

These are the benefits we have because Christ came, died, and rose again. Yet most of us just sit around and have pity parties for ourselves. We stay in the pigpen because we're afraid to face certain situations or stand up to them.

There's no reason to be afraid. Isaiah 54:17 says, *"No weapon formed against you shall prosper."* This verse doesn't say we'll never have a weapon in our face. But it does say a weapon can't prosper when we know who we are in Christ.

And it's not about us anyway. It's about Christ on the inside. He died to take care of all our issues. And He's greater on the inside of us than anything in the world (1 John 4:4). Acts 17:28 says, *"In Him we live and move and have our being."*

Really, we have it easy. We just have to remember what's been provided.

YOU CAN BE FREE

So many people today are struggling in the battlefield of their own minds. They struggle with doing the right thing— even though they know what to do. And they struggle because people are telling them, "It's about the rules. It's about this. It's about that."

The truth is, it's not about anything but a relationship with the living God. It's about knowing that if God is for you, no one can be against you (Rom. 8:31). It's about knowing that being in Christ makes you different from those who aren't. It's not about rules! Jesus didn't come to deliver rules. He came to deliver love, compassion, mercy, and freedom.

Second Corinthians 3:17 says, *"Now the Lord is the Spirit; and where the Spirit of the Lord is, there is liberty."* The *New Living Translation* says, *"there is freedom."*

Where is the Spirit of the Lord? On the inside of us. That means there's freedom on the inside of us. But if we don't understand this, we won't see that freedom on the outside. We'll stay in bondage to things that Christ has set us free from.

Galatians 5:1 tells us, *"Stand fast therefore in the liberty* [or the freedom] *by which Christ has made us free, and do not be entangled again with a yoke of bondage."* This means that even when we open the door for Jesus to live in our hearts (Rev. 3:20), we still may not always do things right. We could still be in bondage. Why? Because we've also got to lean to the inside. We've got to listen to the Lord so we can truly live. We must choose to think like Christ. We must get in the Word and renew our minds—every day.

RENEW YOUR MIND

In Romans 12:2 the Apostle Paul tells us, *"Do not be conformed to this world, but BE TRANSFORMED BY THE RENEWING OF YOUR MIND."* And in Second Corinthians 4:16 he says, *"Even though our outward man is perishing, yet the inward man is being renewed DAY BY DAY."*

I've never understood why some Christians think they don't have to renew their minds every day when Paul said we did. Let's face it. Our minds are not always going to think the right things. In fact, even in situations where we do eventually get it right, our first thought may not have been a God thought.

That's why it's so important to get in the Word every day. Then it won't matter what it looks like on the outside. It won't matter that there seems to be no way out. Because on the inside, we'll know that Christ has made us free. And by faith we can bring that freedom to the outside. As my grandfather always said, "God said it, I believe it, and that settles it for me." If it's settled, it's done.

THE THREE LITTLE PIGS

Do you remember the story of the three little pigs? The big, bad wolf came to huff and puff and blow their houses down. If those little pigs had known about Jesus, they could have spoken to that wolf. But they didn't know the authority they had in Him.

I think a lot of us feel like those three little pigs when the devil comes along. He's huffing and puffing, trying to blow our house down. He wants to defeat us. He wants us to feel like we're losers. We get upset when he comes, because we don't realize that all we have to do is say, "In the Name of Jesus, you have no right, Devil. You have no authority to blow my house down. You have no authority to tear up my life."

It's time to decide that enough is enough. It's time for us to act on the Word and make Jesus Christ a reality in our lives. We don't have to let the devil blow our house down and mess up our life. We can walk in the authority we have in Christ and get out of the pigpen.

See, it's not just about us having eternal life. It's about us knowing that we can have better things here on the earth, because Jesus said, "I came so you could have life and have it more abundantly" (John 10:10).

No matter what pigpen we're in—no matter what it feels or looks like—we can have life and peace when we think like God thinks (Rom. 8:6). We can have an abundant life—we can finish our race with joy (Acts 20:24)—when we realize what we have on the inside.

>> **WE HAVE LIFE-CHANGING ABILITY INSIDE OF US!**

We have life-changing ability inside of us! And because Jesus died on the cross and took the stripes on His back—because He lives—we don't have to be afraid. When we get knocked down, we can jump back up in His Name!

It's time for you to get up. Don't get stuck having a pity party. Start to declare who you are in Christ, rise up from the mud, and live the life God wants you to have!

THINK IT OVER

1. What does it mean to have the mind of Christ?

2. Are there benefits you have in Christ that you aren't using right now? What are they? What can you do to grab hold of them?

3. What have you been thinking about lately? Are you thinking like God thinks or like the world thinks? What can you do to change your thoughts?

4. The Bible says that Christ has made you free. What has He freed you from? What can you do to experience this freedom for yourself?

Chapter 6

BECOME A CHAMPION

"Brethren, I do not count myself to have apprehended;
but one thing I do, forgetting those things which are behind
and reaching forward to those things which are ahead,
I press toward the goal for the prize of the upward
call of God in Christ Jesus."
—Philippians 3:13–14

I love what the Apostle Paul wrote in these verses. Notice that he said *"forgetting those things which are behind."* This scripture tells us that we can forget about everything that's behind us—both the good and the bad. It's not about what we've done. It's about what we're doing now in Christ. And what we should be doing is living an abundant life in Him.

Jesus died and rose from the grave for us. Because He did, we have a wonderful inheritance. And we have the opportunity to change our destiny.

Change isn't always easy, but we don't have to do it in our own strength. Philippians 4:13 says we can do all things through Christ Who gives us strength. Romans 8:37 says, *"In all these things we are more than conquerors through*

>> CHRIST GIVES US STRENGTH AND ABILITY. THROUGH HIM WE ARE MORE THAN CONQUERORS.

Him who loved us." Christ gives us strength and ability. Through Him we are more than conquerors. Where we are weak, He is strong. He's a secret weapon on the inside of us! But we must lay aside every weight and put our focus on Him.

HEBREWS 12:1–2

1 Therefore we also, since we are surrounded by so great a cloud of witnesses, let us LAY ASIDE EVERY WEIGHT, and the sin which so easily ensnares us, and let us run with endurance the race that is set before us,

2 LOOKING UNTO JESUS, the author and finisher of our faith, who for the joy that was set before Him endured the cross, despising the shame, and has sat down at the right hand of the throne of God.

You see, many people have lost their focus. They've gotten caught up in sin or in looking at their circumstances. They've lost their joy and are miserable day after day. Some of them aren't even running their race anymore.

If you ever get to this point—if you ever feel as if you're in the pigpen, far away from God—remember the Word. Come to your senses. This is not a game. This is life. And you have so much potential on the inside.

DEAL WITH IT

It's time for you to lay aside the weight. It's time for you to forget about what's behind you and around you and press toward the mark—toward your future. God's a good God. He loves you so much, and He sees you as a conqueror.

Yes, things are going to happen. You might start to feel frustrated and worthless. You may feel as if you'll never measure up. And you might think, "I've just got to leave. I've got to go out and do my own thing."

Don't let the devil lie to you. Don't let him win. You don't have to have a pigpen experience—a wilderness experience. You don't have to run away from God and rebel. That will only cause you to lose your joy and peace. And the Bible says the wages of sin is death (Rom. 6:23).

Instead, choose to deal with whatever it is that's causing your unhappiness and frustration. Don't let it boil and fester or you'll become like the prodigal son and walk out the door. And that's an issue. Do you really want to let the circumstances change you instead of you changing the circumstances?

The Bible tells us not to be moved by what we see or feel. We should only be moved by what we believe (2 Cor. 5:7).

And we believe that Jesus Christ changed those circumstances 2,000 years ago.

Whether we feel like they've changed or not, whether it looks like they've changed or not, we have to know deep down on the inside that things have changed. It's about living by faith. Where does faith come from? Faith comes by hearing God's Word (Rom. 10:17). When we get away from God's Word, we start lacking faith. And when we lack faith, we're not going to be successful in life. We'll never accomplish anything.

We must believe we can do it. We must build up our faith—not just when things are falling apart, but when things are going good.

Squirrels gather and store up nuts for the winter. And we must do the same with the Word. We must store it up on the inside by renewing our minds. Then, when tough seasons come our way, we'll be prepared. We'll have a relationship with our Heavenly Father. We'll know Him, and we'll know what to do in every battle. We *will* overcome.

RISE UP

Sometimes, despite our best intentions, we still end up in the pigpen. We may not even know how we got there. It's like we're in a fog and the next thing we know we're in the middle of it, surrounded by pigs, and with mud on our face. Our world has been rocked and we don't know what to do.

No matter where we find ourselves or how we got there, we can rise up and become champions once again. We only have to realize that the devil has no right to defeat us, and then come back to our Father—just as the prodigal son did.

"But I just can't take it anymore," some people may say. Then quit taking it! Quit having a pity party in life and let the Greater One on the inside of you help you get up. Rise up in the Name of Jesus! In Christ we are winners, not losers. And victorious people don't lie on the ground and cry. Victorious people don't think, "What am I going to do?" Victorious people shout and rejoice!

> **QUIT HAVING A PITY PARTY IN LIFE AND LET THE GREATER ONE ON THE INSIDE OF YOU HELP YOU GET UP.**

I'm telling you, wherever you are right now, GET UP! Quit letting circumstances get you down! Quit letting problems keep you down. Quit being an emotional mess. Quit looking at everything that's happening around you and start looking at Jesus Christ—your Savior. He is the Answer to every test you're going through. And He is saying, "Get up!"

Don't pray about it anymore. Don't think about it anymore. Just get up! Jesus did not die on the cross for you to just sit around in defeat. He died on the cross so you could get up and go out and fulfill what He called you to do. It's time to arise and shout! It's time to move into what God has for you.

YOU ARE VALUABLE

Our Father God sees you as valuable and precious, even when you don't think you are. He always accepts you. Nothing you can do will separate you from His love. You may have been sleeping with the pigs. You may have lost everything like our prodigal Steve did. But you'll never lose your Heavenly Father. And if

> JESUS DID NOT DIE ON THE CROSS FOR YOU TO JUST SIT AROUND IN DEFEAT. HE DIED ON THE CROSS SO YOU COULD GET UP AND GO OUT AND FULFILL WHAT HE CALLED YOU TO DO.

you have Him, you have everything you need. He'll put you back in right standing—as if you never left. He'll wipe your slate clean. He will lead and guide you in the way you should go.

It's amazing how good God is. He doesn't want you to have crummy, pigpen years. He wants you to prosper and be in health. And He's given you the ability to change your destiny.

Don't be stupid like Steve, our prodigal, and stay trapped in the pigpen. Don't waste the wonderful inheritance that Jesus has given you. He didn't come for you to live life feeling trapped. He didn't come for you to live inadequately, just existing. Jesus came so you could live abundantly! He came so you could have a rich and satisfying life (John 10:10 NLT)!

Dare to live that life. Dare to rise up from the pigpen and become the champion God created you to be. He is always for you, He is always with you, and your best days are ahead!

THINK IT OVER

Are there areas of your life you've let slide into the pigpen? God can take your mess and turn it into something good! It's time to rise up and press forward with Him. Say the following prayer out loud:

God,

Thank You for being my Father. Thank You for loving me, even when I don't always do things right. I realize now that You are full of compassion, mercy, and forgiveness toward me. And I believe that Jesus came so that I could live an abundant life. God, I want to live that life. I want to be the person You want me to be. Help me. Help me to make adjustments. Help me to watch my thought life and to see myself as You see me—complete in Christ. Help me to watch my attitudes—toward people and situations. Help me to pull away from those things in my life that are not of You. And help me to love people as You love people. Give me compassion for those who are hurting. God, I ask You to help me be a light to this dark world. I trust You to lead and guide me. I trust You with every area of my life. I love You. In Jesus' Name I pray, amen.

DO YOU KNOW JESUS?

If you've never accepted Jesus as your Savior, or you need to come back to Him, that's the first step to getting out of the pigpen. Say the following prayer out loud:

God,

I come to You in Jesus' Name. I admit that I'm lost and need help in life. The Bible says, *"If you confess with your mouth that Jesus is Lord and believe in your heart that God raised him from the dead, you will be saved"* (Rom. 10:9 ESV). I believe in my heart that You raised Jesus, Your Son, from the dead. And I confess Him as my Lord. Therefore, according to Your Word, I am saved. I look to You to take care of me—to lead me and guide me. Show me where to go and what to do. Show me how to live for You. In Jesus' Name, amen.

Welcome to God's family! I believe that from this moment on, your life is changing for the better. I want to send you some free materials to help you get started with this new life. Just email **partnerservice@rhema.org** or call **1-866-312-0972**. I want to hear from you!

START DECLARING:
CONFESSIONS TO LIVE BY

Nothing can separate me from God's love (Rom. 8:38–39).

›››

God made me alive with Christ (Eph. 2:5). Jesus took my
punishment—what I deserved—and gave me
His love, joy, health, and peace.

›››

I am more than a conqueror through Christ Jesus
(Rom. 8:37). No situation can keep me down.
He gives me strength and ability.

›››

All of my needs are met in Christ (Phil. 4:19).
I never lack money. I never lack ability.

›››

Jesus took the stripes on His back for my healing
(1 Peter 2:24). I am healed and whole—not
tomorrow or next week, but right now!

›››

God loves me. And He always gives me
the victory through Jesus (1 Cor. 15:57).

》》》

I am full of joy. I rejoice in the Lord always. Devil, you can't defeat me, because the joy of the Lord is my strength (John 16:24; Phil. 4:4; Neh. 8:10).

》》》

I am full of peace. I don't have to worry or be anxious, because in Christ I have the peace that surpasses all understanding (John 14:27; Phil. 4:7).

》》》

In Him—in Christ—I live and move and have my being (Acts 17:28).

》》》

I can do all things through Christ Who strengthens me (Phil. 4:13). There is nothing I can't accomplish in Him.

》》》

God is for me! And because He's for me,
no one can be against me (Rom. 8:31).

》》》

No matter what's going on around me,
I keep my focus on Jesus. I look to Him. He is the
Author and Finisher of my faith (Heb. 12:2).

》》》》

I am not moved by what I see or feel.
I am moved only by what I believe (2 Cor. 5:7).

》》》》

I give all my worries and cares to God, because
He cares about me (1 Peter 5:7).

》》》》

I trust in the Lord with all my heart. I do not lean on my
own understanding. I acknowledge Him in all my ways,
and He directs my paths (Prov. 3:5–6).

》》》》

Jesus came so that I could have life,
and have it more abundantly (John 10:10).

》》》》

I love God with all my heart, soul, mind, and strength.
And I love my neighbor as myself (Mark 12:30–31).
I choose to be a light to this dark and hurting world.

》》》》

I forget those things that are behind me and reach forward
to what's ahead. I press toward the goal for the prize of
the upward call of God in Christ Jesus (Phil. 3:13–14).

"What should I do with my life?"

If you've been asking yourself this question, **RHEMA BIBLE TRAINING COLLEGE is a good place to come and find out.** RBTC will build a solid biblical foundation in you that will carry you through—wherever life takes you.

The Benefits:

◆ Training at *the* **top Spirit-filled Bible school**

◆ Teaching based on steadfast faith in God's Word

◆ Unique two-year core program specially designed to **grow** you as a believer, help you **recognize the voice of God**, and equip you to **live successfully**

◆ Optional **specialized training** in the third- and fourth-year program of your choice: Biblical Studies, Helps Ministry, Itinerant Ministry, Pastoral Ministry, Student Ministries, Worship, World Missions, and General Extended Studies

◆ **Accredited** with Transworld Accrediting Commission International

◆ Worldwide **ministry opportunities**— while you're in school

Apply today!
1-888-28-FAITH (1-888-283-2484)
rbtc.org

Always on.

For the latest news and information on products, media, podcasts, study resources, and special offers, visit us online 24 hours a day.

Free Subscription!

Call now to receive a free subscription to *The Word of Faith* magazine from Kenneth Hagin Ministries. Receive encouragement and spiritual refreshment from . . .

- *Faith-building articles from Kenneth W. Hagin, Lynette Hagin, Craig W. Hagin, and others*

- *"Timeless Teaching" from the archives of Kenneth E. Hagin*

- *Feature articles on prayer and healing*

- *Testimonies of salvation, healing, and deliverance*

- *Children's activity page*

- *Updates on Rhema Bible Training College, Rhema Bible Church, and other outreaches of Kenneth Hagin Ministries*

Subscribe today for your free *Word of Faith*!

1-888-28-FAITH (1-888-283-2484)

rhema.org/wof

OFFER CODE—BKORD:WF